GENETIC DISEASES
AND GENE THERAPIES

BIPOLAR
DISORDER

Richard Spilsbury

rosen publishing's
rosen
central

New York

Published in 2019 by The Rosen Publishing Group, Inc.
29 East 21st Street
New York, NY 10010

Produced for Rosen by Calcium
Editors for Calcium: Sarah Eason and Kris Hirschmann
Designer: Simon Borrough
Picture researcher: Rachel Blount

Photo credits: Cover: Shutterstock: AJP: left; Ase: right; Andrii Muzyka: bottom; Inside: Shutterstock: Africa Studio: p. 41; Andrey Popov: p. 24; Andriano.cz: p. 6; Gorb Andrii: pp. 12-13; Arka38: p. 26; CrispyPork: p. 14; Daisy Daisy: p. 21r; George Dolgikh: p. 43; Eakkaluktemwanich: p. 23; Eranicle: p. 11t; FGC: pp. 4-5, Janson George: p. 39; Martin Charles Hatch: p. 8; Hidesy: p. 38; Kathy Hutchins: p. 45; Icsnaps: p. 7; Iordani: p. 16; Junpinzon: p. 29; Denis Kuvaev: pp. 18-19; Mara008: p. 17; Alex Mit: pp. 10-11b; Natali Mis: p. 35; Nobeastsofierce: p. 36; Orla: p. 21b; Pandora Studio: p. 27; PosiNote: p. 31; Rdonar: p. 32; Ekachai Sathittaweechai: p. 25; Anant Thong: p. 33; Undrey: p. 30; Wavebreakmedia: pp. 20, 44; Mahathir Mohd Yasin: p. 42; Yatso: p. 37.

Cataloging-in-Publication Data

Names: Spilsbury, Richard.
Title: Bipolar disorder / Richard Spilsbury.
Description: New York : Rosen Central, 2019. | Series: Genetic diseases and gene therapies | Includes glossary and index.
Identifiers: LCCN ISBN 9781508182696 (pbk.) | ISBN 9781508182689 (library bound)
Subjects: LCSH: Manic-depressive illness—Juvenile literature. | Manic-depressive illness—Treatment—Juvenile literature. | Teenagers—Mental health—Juvenile literature.
Classification: LCC RC516.S646 2019 | DDC 616.89'5—dc23

Manufactured in the United States of America

Contents

Chapter 1

What Is Bipolar Disorder?

What gets you in a good mood? It might be a nice time with your friends and family, helping someone out, or experiencing something you have hoped to do for a long time, such as seeing your favorite band. Good moods are great, but it is entirely normal to have bad moods, too. We all get down when something doesn't go our way or if our friends let us down, and we may get worried about something that could happen.

Very High, Very Low

Your high and low moods may feel pretty extreme. You might feel so elated or so down that everything else doesn't seem to matter. These powerful moods may even swing from one to another in a short time period. However, some people have swings in mood that are extremely severe. The changes in mood from high to low can totally dominate their lives and make them feel scarily out of control. These people have bipolar disorder.

In the Mind

Bipolar disorder is a mental health condition or mental illness. This means it is caused by how our brains make us feel and react. Mental health conditions range from phobias, such as fear of spaces or spiders, to anxiety, or worrying excessively about things. They vary from bipolar disorder to schizophrenia, which affects how people feel, think, and act in ways that can be harmful to themselves and others. We can sometimes see if someone has a physical illness such as measles or a broken leg, but mental illnesses are often less obvious. However, they can make anyone feel just as bad, or worse, than a physical illness. Like some physical illnesses, bipolar disorder can get passed from parents to children through their genes. Mental health conditions are surprisingly common. Overall, around one in five adults in the United States has a mental illness.

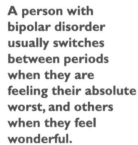

A person with bipolar disorder usually switches between periods when they are feeling their absolute worst, and others when they feel wonderful.

GENE STORIES

"When I am manic it is like I am a superhero. I feel like everything I say is smarter and funnier than anyone else, that I am quicker, more agile, and livelier than the rest. I feel like I'm on top of the world. But during the depressions I feel trapped by how low I feel. I can get so sad and troubled that I feel almost completely cut off from other people, including my friends and family who care about me."

—*Adam, age thirty*

Depressive episodes can trap people in a desolate, sad mood for days or weeks.

Depression and Mania

People with bipolar disorder experience periods of several days or more when they are stuck in one mood. These periods are called episodes. Depressive episodes are periods when someone feels incredibly low with little energy. Manic episodes are periods when someone feels incredibly high and bursting with energy. People with bipolar disorder may experience both of these episode types, but also periods with less extreme mania.

Depressive Episodes

A typical depressive episode can last many days or even weeks. People with bipolar disorder experience a range of emotional responses when they are depressed. After all, all individuals can have their feelings triggered, or caused or set off, by a wide variety of things. Everyone experiences things differently. However, during depressive episodes, most people feel:

- Upset and tearful
- Agitated and tense
- Low self-esteem and poor confidence in their abilities and appearance
- Worthlessness
- Guilt
- Lack of enjoyment, even in things they usually like to do
- Exhaustion and deep tiredness
- Uninterested in food and exercise

During depressive episodes, some people feel like punishing or even harming themselves. Others turn to drugs and alcohol in an attempt to ease their painful feelings.

Manic Episodes

Manic episodes are totally different from depressive episodes. These episodes last a week or more. People feel a range of sometimes astonishing highs. Someone experiencing a manic episode is often:

- Incredibly happy, laughing, and telling jokes
- Unusually friendly, or rude or aggressive to others
- Overexcited or agitated
- Distracted, with poor concentration
- Very active and wakeful
- Taking risks—they are not only adventurous, but also put themselves in dangerous situations
- Talkative—they may speak a lot and also at high speed, without making much sense
- Not shy and prepared to do unusual or inappropriate things

During manic episodes people may spend lots of money and make all sorts of promises to do things. Afterward, some people may remember things that happened in an episode and feel unhappy or ashamed about things they have done. Others may remember virtually none of what happened. People usually feel exhausted after a manic episode.

A less severe form of mania is hypomania. Episodes last less than a week and feel more manageable. That is because people can still carry on with normal daily life even if they are feeling overexcited, full of energy, and so on.

When mania strikes, people often become supercharged with energy and happiness.

Types of Bipolar Disorder

In the past, bipolar disorder used to be called manic depression because people thought there were always separate episodes of mania and depression. Now, doctors usually avoid describing someone as a manic depressive because they may get hypomanic rather than manic episodes, have overlapping lows and highs, or rarely experience deep depressions. Bipolar disorder is a better term for covering the whole range of different combinations of moods that different sufferers experience.

Doctors usually describe five types of bipolar disorder, based on the types of episodes that a person experiences. People will also experience neutral periods between episodes in which they have a normal range of emotions, but no mania, hypomania, or depression.

Bipolar I: severe episodes of mania and depression,

The life course of someone with bipolar disorder is a roller coaster of powerful emotions.

including at least one episode of mania lasting longer than a week

Bipolar II: a lengthy episode of severe depression, often lasting several months, and milder, shorter episodes of hypomania

Cyclothymia: a blend of brief episodes of both depression and hypomania; episodes are less severe than in Bipolar II, but occur fairly regularly over two years or more

Mixed features: both manic or hypomanic and depressive moods and symptoms at the same time during the same episodes, such as high energy and despair

Rapid cycling: a speeded-up form of bipolar disorder in which people experience four or more mood episodes of at least several days each, in a twelve-month period; sometimes moods can switch from high to low within a day

GENE STORIES

"Rapid cycling is tough to deal with. It feels like a large roller coaster that is never-ending. I don't know how long, how often, how high or deep the highs and lows are going to be. There's deep depression as you fall, and happiness when you're climbing, but always anxiety when you approach the top."
—*Vikram, age forty*

Some people have mental health conditions that share some symptoms with bipolar disorder. For example, someone with obsessive compulsive disorder, or OCD, has obsessions such as cleanliness or tidiness, anxiety when things are out of place or possibly dirty, and a compulsion, or a strong desire or need, to do things such as clean or tidy up. Some of these symptoms are found in some people's hypomanic episodes. If someone with OCD has periods of deep depression, too, then it could be a bit like Bipolar II. Some doctors think there is a bipolar spectrum, in which people with bipolar disorder also have other mental conditions. Others think these other conditions are separate, with different causes and treatments.

Chapter 2

Why Do People Develop Bipolar Disorder?

During bipolar episodes, people experience a blend of overwhelming changes to their regular mood, sleep patterns, energy, thoughts, and behavior. For some people, episodes come on gradually over several days. For others, the episodes can start with little warning. However they experience their illness, the root cause of the intense moods in people with bipolar disorder is their brain.

The Brain

The brain is the headquarters of the nervous system. This is a network of nerves that carry information to and from the rest of your body. Nearly everything we do is controlled by our brains. For example, your brain instructs your muscles to move your limbs, allows you to react to pain, and lets you enjoy music you hear. Each brain contains about 100 billion nerve cells called neurons. They are not just packed together in a big jumble. They are organized into different areas forming parts with different jobs to do.

Cerebrum: allows us to respond to the world around us; the front part controls thinking and speaking, and the back part controls vision

Cerebellum: controls coordination of movement, such as keeping balance

Brain stem: controls essential and automatic functions that need to happen day and night, such as moving your lungs to breathe and keeping your heart beating

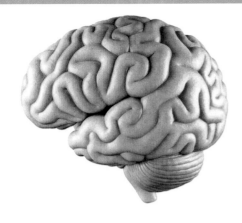

A human brain is pink and gray and wrinkly, with the texture of the white of a boiled egg. It weighs around 3 pounds (1.4 kilograms) and is protected inside your skull.

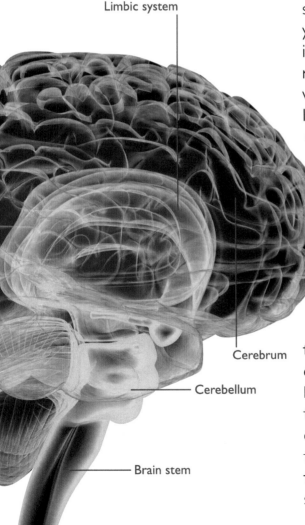

Limbic system

Cerebrum

Cerebellum

Brain stem

Limbic System

Have you ever felt a strong desire to do something daring, such as rock-climbing or singing on stage, even though you are afraid you will fail? The limbic system is a collection of brain parts responsible for all the emotions we feel and things we remember. It makes us feel motivated to do things and experience fear. It is constantly updating new memories of experiences; linking tastes and sights with pleasant memories; and rules of how to behave, including emotional reactions; and moderating feelings of anger. The limbic system also detects if we are thirsty, hungry, getting too hot, or need to sleep. Studies of the brains of people with bipolar disorder have revealed that their limbic systems function differently than people without the disorder. This is the brain part that makes a difference in whether someone has the disorder or not.

Brain Messengers

Have you ever played telephone, the game where someone whispers a phrase quietly to one person, who whispers it to the next person, and so on? Often, the phrase heard by the last person is very different from what the first person said. In people with bipolar disorder, the parts of their limbic system fail to communicate normally with one another. Messages get lost in translation, so they can get misinterpreted. That means that the limbic system has less control of feelings and responses to emotions. To understand how this happens, we need to look at how messages move in the nervous system and brain.

Nerves and Neurons

We can think of nerves like telephone cables containing bundles of thin wires running through the body. Each wire

Noradrenaline is the neurotransmitter controlling fear and excitement. It is in high supply when you are on a roller coaster. For many animals, noradrenaline can spur them to fight for survival.

is a chain of neurons. Bundles of neurons in nerves constantly carry messages to and from different parts of the body. Neurons are special cells with a long part called an axon on one side, and tufty parts called dendrites on the other. Nerve messages move as tiny, very fast bursts of electricity through the axon of one neuron. At the end, they reach a very small gap called a synapse before the start of the dendrites of the next neuron. The messages cross over this synapse using special chemicals that act as messengers. These are called neurotransmitters. The message gets passed on through the chain of neurons in this way.

Different Neurotransmitters

Neurons in the brain do not always make the same neurotransmitter. They make different ones, each with a special meaning. Scientists think that bipolar disorder is caused when three neurotransmitters called noradrenaline, serotonin, and dopamine are produced in abnormal amounts. Then messages getting to parts of the limbic system become distorted. For example, too little or too much dopamine in the limbic system disrupts normal feelings of pleasure and emotional reward, as well as logical thought patterns. Imbalance of serotonin affects sleepiness, ability to learn and remember, and mood.

GENE STORIES

"I can't understand why people take drugs. My bipolar feels like there is a permanent pharmacy in my head. It starts dispensing chemicals with little warning that can either give me scary highs or scary lows. Who would want to risk doing that to themselves?"

—*Lucy, age nineteen*

Triggers

Bipolar disorder is an illness that people have for life. Often, it begins when people are in their twenties, but some people may be affected younger and others won't start to see symptoms until they are much older. The reasons people begin to experience episodes are quite varied, but often there are triggers that lead to them.

Stress and Trauma

You probably know someone whose moods and emotions have been thrown into chaos. Perhaps this person broke up with someone, or had deep money worries. Bipolar disorder can be triggered by stressful life events, but also by ongoing stress such as very low self-esteem. Traumatic, or deeply upsetting or disturbing, life-changing events are even more likely to trigger bipolar episodes. These can include being bullied or abused by others, witnessing

Serious accidents, and thoughts of survival and death, can trigger initial bipolar episodes.

a horrific event such as a car crash, losing a loved one, or being seriously injured. Low moods, lack of sleep and appetite, and other changes caused by stress and trauma may trigger bipolar episodes.

Hormonal Changes

The brain needs chemical messengers to function, but the rest of the body also uses chemicals called hormones to communicate and change. For example, at puberty, the pituitary gland at the base of our brain makes and releases growth hormones, which make us start to grow. The thyroid glands in the neck produces the thyroid hormone. When a thyroid produces unusually low levels of this hormone, a person can experience depression, whereas high levels elevate moods. In some women, changing hormone levels after giving birth can also trigger bipolar disorder.

Seasons

Some people start to experience bipolar disorder as a result of changing light levels in different seasons. Long, dark winters can trigger depressive episodes, and sunnier, lighter conditions in spring and summer trigger manic or hypomanic episodes. Such changes are the result of the body's biological or body clock, which is our internal response to changes in light and dark through every twenty-four-hour period and throughout the year. People with Seasonal Affective Disorder (SAD) also become depressed in winter, but do not experience manic episodes.

GENE STORIES

"My bipolar episodes come and go like clockwork. Every spring, I cycle into a manic state for about four months, until a depression cycle comes along in August, possibly related to the start of college. I become stable in October and stay that way until January, when I find myself in a depression until spring. But I have more manic than depressive episodes now that I live in California than when I lived in gloomy Ohio."

—Gina, age twenty-one

Chapter 3

Bipolar Disorder and Genes

The chemicals responsible for bipolar disorder are made by cells. Cells are the building blocks of any living thing. The way any cell develops, grows, and functions depends on the instructions found inside it. We call these instructions genes. The role of a gene includes what and how much chemical it produces. Experts believe that the chances of someone developing bipolar disorder depends partly on their genes.

Inside Genes

Genes are made up of a substance called deoxyribonucleic acid (DNA). It looks a little like a ladder twisted into a spiral. Each rung of the ladder is made from a particular sequence of chemicals, like a string of letters completing a word. Words in a book of instructions can tell us what to do, just as the genetic code of chemicals in DNA can instruct cells. A person's genes contain all the instructions for living that they will ever need. However, only the genes that have any effect are the ones that are actually turned on. This means their instructions become active. Some genes never become active. The gene instructions involved in bipolar disorder are in everyone. But the genes become active in only around 1 percent of people, who then develop bipolar disorder.

Genes are responsible for everything about a person. This ranges from eye or hair color to what illnesses or conditions that person may develop.

Just one chromosome has about fifty million different chemicals. Their patterns are a genetic code of instructions that tell cells what to do.

GENE STORIES

Magdalena sank into a long, deep depression after weeks of feeling good about herself. She was diagnosed and lived with bipolar disorder for many years. Then, Magdalena saw an ad calling for people with bipolar disorder to take part in a genetic study. She donated some blood and scientists studied the DNA it contained. Based on Magdalena's sample, and the samples of many other people, scientists figured out that the disorder may involve a gene called ANK3. Magdalena said, "If you have cardiac disease, you can do things to stop it getting worse, like exercising loads. But bipolar disorder is just there, so it really helped to get involved in the study and make a difference to others with the same condition."

Chromosome Mix

Thousands of genes are twisted and packed tightly into chromosomes inside cells. Each cell in our bodies contains twenty-three pairs of chromosomes, making forty-six altogether. When living things reproduce sexually, one chromosome of each pair from a male joins with another from a female to produce new pairs in their offspring. Each person inherits, or receives from their mother and father, a unique set of chromosomes with its own combination of genes. Particular mixes of genes can make it more likely for a person to develop a particular illness.

Genes and Medical Conditions

If your mother has brown eyes and your father has blue eyes, you probably have brown eyes even though you inherited genes for each color. That's because the brown version is dominant, or more powerful, and the blue version is recessive, or can be masked, so it takes a back seat to the brown color form. There are different forms because of changes or mutations in the code of the DNA in the eye color gene. Many medical conditions are caused by mutations in genes.

Mutations can happen when DNA is not copied properly as cells divide during growth and reproduction. They can also happen when people are exposed to harmful chemicals. For example, chemicals in smoke can damage DNA and cause mutations in lung cells causing cancer. Some mutations are neutral and have no effect, some are beneficial, and others can cause a disease.

Some genetic diseases, such as cystic fibrosis, can only happen if a child inherits the same mutation from each parent. If a person has cystic fibrosis, his or her lungs become clogged with thick, sticky mucus. If someone inherits just one copy of the cystic fibrosis gene from a parent, he or she will be a carrier of the condition but won't actually have it. Other genetic diseases, such as Huntington's disease, are inherited if a child gets even one mutated Huntington's gene from a parent. Still other genetic diseases, such as Down syndrome, are not actually inherited from a parent. Down syndrome happens when, during reproduction, a child gets an extra copy of chromosome 21. These extra instructions result in a set of developmental changes. Scientists do not think that there is a single mutation making people likely to get bipolar disorder, but instead multiple genes interacting together.

Only about 1 percent of people born with Down syndrome inherited the condition from their parents. The rest got the condition after random changes in their parents' chromosomes.

Gene Genies

Scientists are on the hunt for the genes involved in bipolar disorder. They look for segments of DNA on particular chromosomes that are always inherited by people who have the disease but not by people who do not. These mutations are likely playing their part in the disease. So far, scientists suspect that parts of chromosomes 12 and 21 are most likely involved. Part of their evidence is that people with Down syndrome almost never develop mania, probably because the extra copy of the chromosome protects against bipolar disorder.

Running in the Family

It has taken many, many years for scientists to discover that bipolar disorder can be caused by someone's particular genetic makeup. Key to establishing this has been finding that bipolar disorder often runs in families.

Patterns of Illness

Scientists and doctors study populations of people and examine medical records to find patterns of illness so they can figure out causes and treatments. To find out if a disease has genetic causes, they focus on patterns of illness in families to estimate their heritability. Heritability is the likelihood that the cause of the illness is due to genes. If one family member has an illness, and there is a higher heritability of the same disease in the family than in people in the general population, then it is likely that genes are playing a significant role in the spread of the condition.

Many studies of bipolar patients and their relatives have shown that bipolar disorder runs in families. The most convincing genetic data comes from studies of identical twins. Scientists report that if one identical twin has bipolar disorder, the other twin has around a 50 percent chance of developing the condition.

Researchers have discovered that an identical twin of a bipolar twin has about a 50 percent chance of also developing bipolar disorder in their lifetime.

Why Twins?

The reason studies of twins are important to people researching the spread of disorders and diseases is that twins share some of their genes. Identical twins share all of their genes, whereas non-identical twins share half. It stands to reason that if one identical twin develops the same condition as his or her twin, then it is likely that genes have had something to do with it. If they have not yet developed the condition, then their chances of doing so are higher than if they were non-identical twins or just regular siblings who are not twins.

Gene Genies

Research studies have established the importance of heritability in bipolar disorder. In one study at Johns Hopkins University, researchers discovered that approximately 40 percent of parents or siblings of bipolar patients also had bipolar disorder. In another study at Stanford University, researchers reported that 51 percent of children of people with bipolar disorder had a psychiatric disorder. These included depression, bipolar disorder, and attention deficit hyperactivity disorder (ADHD). Although links between the other psychiatric conditions and bipolar disorder are not clear, such studies support the role of genes in mental illness.

Scientists believe that studies of heritability of bipolar disorder will help them to locate and treat the genes responsible for its impact on mental health.

Chapter 4

Treating Bipolar Disorder

Before people can get treatment or help for their bipolar disorder, they need a diagnosis. A diagnosis is when doctors or specialists examine a person and identify the symptoms or signs that tell them that person has a particular injury, disease, or condition.

Talking About It

When someone goes to the doctor with a problem, the doctor may use special blood tests or other forms of physical examination to figure out what is wrong with the patient and give them a diagnosis. Most tests like these are not much help when it comes to diagnosing bipolar disorder. Doctors will do a physical examination, but this is to rule out illnesses or medications that might be causing a person's symptoms. To determine if someone has bipolar disorder, a doctor must talk to the patient and hear about symptoms directly from him or her. That's why it is very important for people to talk honestly and clearly to the doctor about their mood swings, behavior, and what life is like for them day to day. A doctor who diagnoses mental health conditions such as bipolar disorder is called a psychiatrist.

Psychiatrists at Work

A psychiatrist will ask a patient about symptoms, such as mood swings, and will want to know how bad they are, how long they last, and how often they happen. They will also ask how a person feels at the time mood swings happen. Psychiatrists keep careful notes about how regularly mood swings happen because one way to diagnose bipolar disorder is to see that regular episodes of high or low moods are often accompanied by an increase in energy, sleeplessness, and fast thinking or speech. The psychiatrist also asks people about their memory, how well they find they can express themselves, and how their moods affect their relationships.

Background Checks

Before a person with bipolar disorder sees their doctor or psychiatrist, he or she should write down any symptoms that might indicate depression, hypomania, or mania. It also helps if the person spends some time asking relatives about any experiences of personal mental illness, depression, or bipolar disorder. As bipolar disorder is sometimes caused in part by the genes, having a full record of any mental health problems in a family can help with a diagnosis.

Diagnosis of bipolar disorder depends on someone having episodes within a particular timescale. So it's important for patients to keep records of when episodes happen and how long they last, as well as noting how they feel.

Medication

After doctors identify the signs and symptoms of bipolar depression, hypomania, and mania, they can start to help a patient. In most cases, they can treat the disorder effectively and safely with bipolar medications.

The medicines used to treat bipolar disorder cannot cure it or stop it altogether. Instead, they can reduce how bad the episodes of depression and mania feel, and they can reduce the number of times they happen. Some medications are designed to help reduce the extreme ups and downs of mood swings. These are known as mood stabilizers. To reduce episodes of depression, people with bipolar disorder may take medicines called antidepressants, like people with depression do. However, taking antidepressants when you have bipolar disorder can trigger an episode of hypomania, so their use is carefully monitored. Sometimes mood stabilizers will be enough to help control the depression, anyway. If not, patients may also be given a medicine known as an antipsychotic to help control the depression.

Doctors regularly check patients who take medication for bipolar disorder to ensure that the levels of medications they are using are correct and are not affecting their body in a bad way.

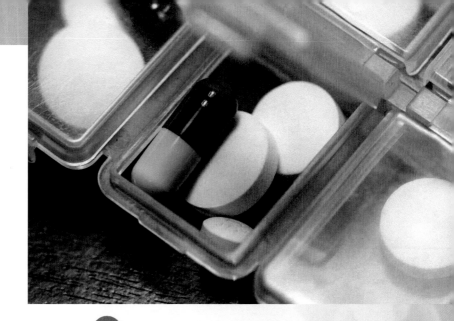

When people are diagnosed with bipolar disorder, it's important that they are fully involved in the decisions about their treatment. This is partly because they will probably need to take medication for the rest of their lives. It's vital for them to understand that they need to keep taking the medications, even at times when they feel better. It's also important that people understand the need for patience, as it can take time to find what medications work for each individual. If one doesn't work well for them, they may have to try several others before finding the right one. After starting medication, it can also take several weeks or even months before a patient starts to feel any benefits.

GENE STORIES

"When the doctor told me I had bipolar disorder it was a huge relief! Finally I had an explanation for all of the strange thoughts I had racing around in my head. At last I knew what I was dealing with. There were medications that could help me. Once I knew what I was dealing with, I knew I could start to manage it. I'd prefer not to have to take two pills every day, but it means I can live my life to the full and enjoy it, so I do."

—Juan, age twenty-three

Behavioral Therapies

As well as medication, sufferers of bipolar disorder can get other kinds of therapies to help them to live as normally as possible. These are often known as behavioral therapies. These usually involve talking one-to-one, with family, or in groups with people who are trained to help others deal with problems such as depression by learning techniques to cope with or control symptoms.

Cognitive Behavioral Therapy

The idea of cognitive behavioral therapy, or CBT, is to help people identify unhealthy, negative ideas and behaviors and replace them with healthy, positive ones. CBT can help people with bipolar disorder figure out what triggers episodes and help them to learn ways of coping with stress and upsetting situations. CBT looks for practical ways to improve a person's state of mind day to day.

CBT therapists help people to break down overwhelming feelings into separate areas, such as situations, thoughts, emotions, physical feelings, and actions. CBT is based on the idea that these different areas are connected; the way people think about a particular situation affects how they feel about it and how they respond or act when it happens. Imagine, for example, a person who hits a problem and thinks, "I'll never be able to sort it out." This person is likely to fail and feel depressed about it.

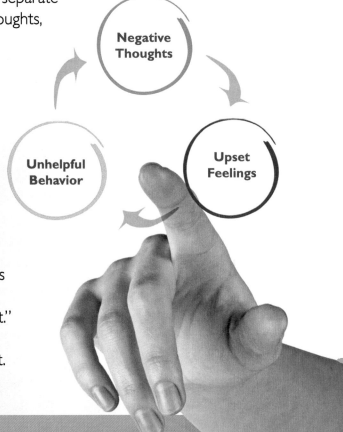

Negative Thoughts

Upset Feelings

Unhelpful Behavior

Family-focused therapists may help parents see how things they think they are doing to help, such as being too controlling of their child because they are worried about them, might actually be making things worse.

On the other hand, a person who realizes that everyone faces problems, and knows that he or she might be able to solve it or get help solving it, is more likely to have a positive outcome. This is an oversimplified example, but it gives you an idea of how therapists can help people look at problems in a helpful rather than unhelpful way.

Family-Focused Therapy

Another example of behavioral therapy that can help people with bipolar disorder is family-focused therapy, or FFT. This therapy helps to teach patients and their families about bipolar disorder so that relatives can help patients stick with their treatment plan and recognize and manage warning signs of mood swings. FFT also helps patients and their families to identify any difficulties and conflicts within the family and show them how those problems might be causing stress for both the patient and the family. Therapists help families to find ways to solve any problems or difficulties they might have, which can be a big help for patients.

Chapter 5

Living with Bipolar Disorder

The first weeks and months after getting a diagnosis of bipolar disorder can be very difficult. People who have been told they have the condition may feel completely overwhelmed at the thought of having a lifelong illness like this. When people are getting successful medication and therapy, they start to see that although bipolar disorder will change the course of their life, it doesn't mean that they can't do the things they want to do. People can help themselves by using different coping strategies along with their medication and therapies.

Different Routes

There is no reason having bipolar disorder should prevent most people from accomplishing their goals. People with bipolar disorder can still get married, get the job they always wanted, and lead productive and successful lives. It may just mean that they have to find different routes or take a little longer to get there. For example, many people diagnosed with bipolar disorder in their twenties continue their studies at college. They may have to take fewer classes every semester, making it take longer for them to graduate, but they still achieve a college degree in the end.

Be Positive

Having bipolar disorder is just a small part of who a person is. It does not define him or her. It's important for people who have bipolar disorder—and everyone else—to understand that there is a difference between the symptoms and the person. Of course, the symptoms will affect a person's behavior, but people can find ways to control those behaviors. The behaviors and symptoms do not define the person. Some people would like others to understand that there are also positives about having a mental health condition such as bipolar disorder. One of the positives is that bipolar disorder often makes people very creative and self-motivated, which helps them to be great at the jobs they choose to do.

Talking About It

Living with bipolar disorder can be challenging, and having people to talk to can make all the difference in how a person feels and copes with their condition. Some people with bipolar disorder feel more comfortable talking to family and friends about their condition and how they are feeling about it. Other people may find it easier to join a support group. These are groups of people who all have the condition. Talking to people who face many similar problems can help people to realize they are not alone. It also gives people the chance to share ideas for coping and to learn from others who understand what they are going through.

Music can have a big impact on mood, and people with bipolar disorder may listen to particular pieces or artists to ease their episodes.

Staying Active and Eating Well

Eating a healthy diet and keeping active are important for everyone, regardless of whether they have a condition such bipolar disorder or not. However, a healthy lifestyle can make a huge difference to people living with bipolar disorder, helping them to stay well and to feel happier and more settled.

Doing regular exercise and planning activities that people enjoy and look forward to creates a sense of achievement.

A healthy lifestyle is one in which a person is regularly physically active, gets adequate amounts of sleep, eats healthy foods, and avoids harmful substances such as alcohol and drugs. If people with bipolar disorder keep themselves fit and healthy, not only does it make them feel better, in some cases it may even reduce their need for medication. All of us should try to do at least thirty minutes of exercise every day. Exercise keeps you fit and makes your body release endorphins. These are feel-good chemicals that boost the mood, which is particularly helpful in reducing the depressive symptoms of someone with bipolar disorder. Exercise also helps people sleep, which helps them to feel better.

A common side effect, or unwanted extra symptom, caused by some medications for bipolar disorder is weight gain. The medications make people put on weight more easily, which can make people depressed and unhealthy. Eating a healthy diet and exercising regularly can limit weight gain. Some medications may also increase the risk of developing diabetes, or worsening the condition in people who already have it. People with bipolar disorder are advised to have regular checkups to monitor their risk of conditions such as diabetes. During a checkup, doctors will record the patient's weight, check blood pressure, and take blood tests. Exercise and a healthy weight reduce the risk of diabetes as well as bipolar disorder.

Fruit and vegetables are an important part of a healthy diet.

Gene Genies

Scientists have discovered that people with bipolar disorder have overly sensitive body clocks, the timekeepers in our bodies that control circadian rhythms. Circadian rhythms tell our bodies when to sleep, wake up, and eat, and they are usually triggered by environmental cues, such as sunlight, darkness, and temperature. When circadian rhythms are stable, a person's mood is more stable, too. A new therapy called interpersonal and social rhythm therapy (IPSRT) helps to reset the body clocks of people with bipolar disorder by establishing a daily routine of regular hours and times for sleeping, exercising, and eating. A consistent routine helps those with bipolar disorder manage their moods better.

Self-Help

One of the most important ways people with bipolar disorder can help themselves is by learning as much as they can about the condition. This can help them manage symptoms and prevent the condition from getting worse. Also, knowing what's going on can help people to make sure they get the support that they need and make a plan to help themselves.

Spotting Triggers

One of the main ways people can help themselves is by learning what triggers an episode to see if they can avoid it or prepare for it better. Some people do this by keeping a chart or making notes in a journal about what they do, what has happened in their day, and how they feel, as well as recording when an episode happens and how bad it is. Many people with bipolar disorder keep records like this their whole

Some people with bipolar disorder find that yoga can have a calming influence on their moods.

lives. By looking back over several months, they can often see what triggers an episode. Using this knowledge, they can find ways to avoid the triggers and reduce the number or severity of the episodes they have. Some people ask relatives to help them spot triggers, as the people who love them may notice that certain things, such as sudden changes in routine, can set them off. If friends and family know what a person's triggers are, they can help that person to avoid them.

Avoiding and Preparing for Triggers

Some triggers, such as changing seasons or hormonal changes, cannot really be avoided, but many can. For example, if a person you know is argumentative and shouts at you, making you stressed, you may be able to choose to avoid that person. For triggers that cannot be avoided, at least if a person knows they are coming, he or she can prepare for them. For example, if being busy at work makes a person stressed, he or she could plan to have plenty of quiet time at home during a busy period so that things don't spiral out of control. That person can also practice ways to unwind, such as breathing exercises or listening to calming music.

GENE STORIES

"One technique that I use to prepare for triggers when they happen is counting backward from a high number. I picture myself writing the numbers down, one after the other, erasing one number before writing the next. Or as I count backward I picture myself walking down a staircase, one step at a time, and each time I walk down a step, I take a deep breath!"
—Malik, age forty-one

Chapter 6

Bipolar Disorder and Gene Therapy

In the future, someone living with bipolar disorder may be able to stop it in its tracks. This is possible because scientists have found ways to swap out mutations that cause illnesses and replace them with healthy versions. This is called gene therapy.

Gene Therapy

Gene therapy targets particular genes in an organism, or living thing. Scientists first carefully identify a mutated section of DNA on a gene that is not functioning properly and might be causing a health problem. They then replace it with a new, functioning gene. The technique of editing, or making changes to, genes was first developed in the 1970s. However, it is only in recent times that improved equipment such as powerful computers and better laboratory techniques for gene editing have been available for scientists to use. Gene therapy is not in use to treat bipolar disorder just yet, but it has already been successful in treating some illnesses.

There are two main types of gene therapy. In one type, DNA is transferred into any cell in an organism that is not a sperm or an egg cell. Then the effects of gene therapy will not be inherited by children of the person being treated. The other type of gene therapy edits genes in sex cells, and therefore changes can be passed on to children from parents.

Knowing Genes

The first step to gene therapy in humans is knowing what genes are inside them, where they are located on chromosomes, and exactly what they do. For example, specific genes may cause cells to make particular proteins that have various functions. In 2001, scientists revealed to the world that they had identified nearly twenty-one thousand genes in every human. This was the result of combined efforts of scientists worldwide in looking at the patterns of around three billion chemical code units in human chromosomes. It had taken around ten years of hard work to discover about 90 percent of the total human genome. The work has continued since then, and experts believe they may eventually discover thirty thousand genes in the genome.

Gene Genies

The first success in gene therapy came in treating a rare condition called severe combined immune deficiency (SCID) back in 2000. Before treatments were available, people born with SCID had to live in protective plastic bubbles because their bodies had no defenses against infections caused by tiny organisms such as bacteria. The treatment edits mutated copies of a gene called adenosine deaminase. In 2016, a safer, more practical version of this SCID gene therapy became available.

Gene editing is a simple idea, but in practice, it is not nearly as simple as using forceps to pull out unwanted genes and replace them with different versions.

How Gene Therapy Works

The idea of gene editing is fairly simple, but, in reality, it is incredibly difficult to splice a piece of DNA into particular cells to change them. Gene therapy uses a person's own cells to treat them, but needs the help of viruses, which are tiny organisms that invade and live in body cells and cause disease.

Virus Messengers

If you have ever had a cold, then you have been attacked by a virus. Viruses are incredibly small living things, much smaller than bacteria. They have a small amount of DNA in genes protected inside a protein layer. Viruses can only reproduce once they get inside other living cells. Once inside, they use energy from the host cell to make hundreds of thousands of copies of their genetic material.

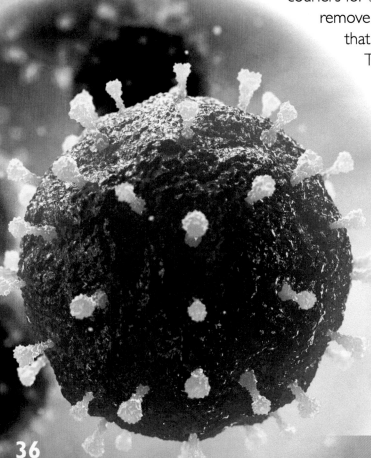

Scientists can use modified viruses as couriers for sections of DNA. They first remove any of the virus's own genes that cause sicknesses in people. Then they replace them with the normal functioning gene to be added in the gene therapy procedure. The virus can then "infect" human cells with this normal gene. The normal version replaces the mutated one.

Viruses are so tiny that millions could fit on a pinhead! The knobs on a virus help it locate and attach to cells.

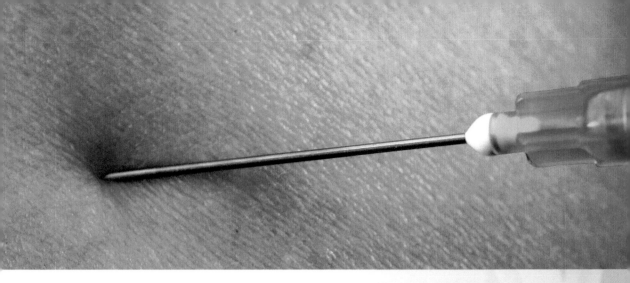

In gene therapy, stem cells containing genes delivered into them by virus messengers are usually injected into people with a needle and syringe.

Where It Happens

Gene therapy happens in laboratories when scientists introduce viruses into special cells called stem cells. These are types of cells that can divide over and over. They produce not only more stem cells, but also cells that can turn into many different types of cells, such as neurons. Scientists can get stem cells from different places around the body, such as bone marrow and skin, but also from the nervous system. Once they have the cells, they add a solution containing the viruses along with chemicals to help the stem cells divide more quickly. After washing off the solutions, scientists can then inject the cells containing the normal gene into the person receiving the gene therapy. Once inside the body, the normal copy of the gene will get passed on to other cells.

Gene Genies

In 2014, scientists took samples of skin cells from people with and without bipolar disorder. They treated the cells to act like stem cells, then turn into neurons. They found that the bipolar neurons passed on signals from one to another in a more confused way than normal neurons. Scientists think this might mean that in people with bipolar disorder, genes in neurons in one part of the brain may act as though they are in another part, and neurotransmitters may mix up messages.

The Challenges of Gene Therapy

Gene therapy is a much more complex way of treating someone with an illness than giving pills or injections of chemicals. The techniques may work well in a laboratory setting, but they are more difficult to predict in patients.

One of the biggest challenges to gene therapy is the body's defensive shield, the immune system. It is operated by a mobile army of white blood cells that defend your body's cells when they detect attack by other organisms, such as viruses. The viruses used in gene therapy can be recognized as intruders, too, even though they are not introducing a harmful disease. When the immune system goes into attack mode, your body uses up lots of energy so you feel exhausted. But it can also cause inflammation, or swelling, of tissue and even failure of organs such as the liver. This is why scientists work hard to find viruses that are less likely to trigger an immune response.

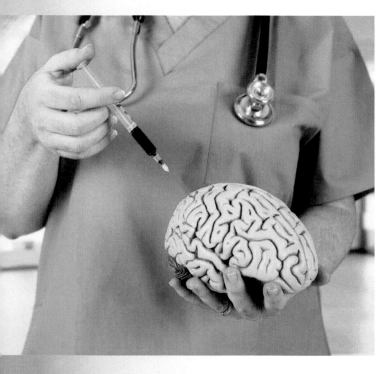

Injecting edited cells into the brain is potentially harmful, as physical damage to delicate tissues in different brain parts could affect the brain's function. Many normal medicines can be injected into the blood, and the body circulates them and the blood around the

A brain is an incredibly delicate organ that can be damaged if injections are given in the wrong places.

body to where they are useful. But there is a barrier between blood and the brain that gene therapy transporters, such as viruses, cannot pass. Another problem is that gene therapy relies on spreading the replacement gene when cells divide and copy themselves. Neurons stop dividing in the brain after about age five.

Gene therapy for bipolar disorder may change behavior in mice or other animals, but may not have the same effect in humans.

Gene Genies

Scientists studying gene functions in mice accidentally edited out a particular gene called NR2E1 on chromosome 6. They noticed that this change made animals unusually aggressive, even killing other mice. When they edited the human version of NR2E1 into mice, the animals became less aggressive. This gene produces proteins that control how other genes work, so it may also have hidden effects on other genes in action in the mice's brains.

Many drug treatments and therapies are tested on animals such as mice to determine if they are safe for use in people. Sometimes when something works in animals, it can fail in people. For example, sleeping pills containing the drug thalidomide were tested on guinea pigs with no harmful effects. But pregnant women taking the drug unexpectedly gave birth to children with shortened limbs.

Why Is Gene Therapy Controversial?

Gene therapy is a very promising approach to dealing with all kinds of illnesses, including mental health problems. However, there are concerns about many aspects of its use.

Scientists are continually researching the location and function of genes in the human genome. They are establishing how different genes work together to control how parts of the body and parts of the brain are interconnected. However, gene therapy relies on accurately delivering genes to particular places, and it is difficult to be on target.

Sections of DNA reach specific targets using gene-editing tools. For example, one tool uses a tiny piece of DNA with a chemical code that matches that of the section of DNA sequence that needs to be edited. It binds to this section, then a protein acts like scissors to cut it out. The problem is that sometimes the tool finds and cuts out similar but not matching sections of unrelated genes. Then it might stop the other gene from working. For example, if the altered gene stops a cell from growing normally, the normal cell might turn into a cancer cell. During early attempts at SCID gene therapy, DNA missed the target and caused a type of cancer called leukemia in several patients being treated.

Many inherited illnesses affect a relatively small number of people. It is expensive to develop and use gene therapy techniques. When there are fewer users of such techniques, they remain expensive and may be unaffordable to some people desperate for gene therapy.

Gene therapy has the potential to treat people with bipolar disorder, but what other changes could this treatment cause them and any future children they may have?

Many people are concerned about how gene therapy changes people's genomes. An improvement in one part of the genome may have unexpected and unintended consequences in other parts. For example, easing manic episodes in people with bipolar disorder may have unexpected effects on their memory, logic, or other processes. They may not like the feel of the new personality they develop.

GENE STORIES

"No doubt it is difficult to live with, but I don't resent having bipolar disorder; it's part of the person I've become. In fact, I'm grateful to the illness for enhancing parts of my life like appreciating art and music. Bipolar is a magnifying glass that sits between me and the world around me."
—*Josefine, age twenty*

Success for Bipolar Disorder Sufferers

Scientists are still studying the options for gene therapy for individuals with bipolar disorder, and it will probably become a reality someday. Someday, it might even be possible to use gene therapy to prevent people from getting a wide range of conditions that currently do not have such options available.

The Promise of Success

Gene therapy, if successful, would mean that the lives of people with bipolar disorder are not punctuated with mood episodes. It could reduce the depths and heights of mania and depression, change mania to hypomania, or even eliminate these swings altogether. It could also mean that people do not need to take medication each day to moderate their moods. People may still face the same triggers that push them along a roller coaster of emotions, but the highs and lows will not be so extreme. Before implementing this treatment, however, scientists and doctors will need to carry out trials to test the safety and effectiveness of gene therapy. Long-term studies on large numbers of people will give a better idea of the long-term impacts the therapy will have on health and brain function.

Individual Therapy

You know how some people can eat dairy foods, but others get sick if they eat milk or cheese? Everyone reacts differently to the things that go into their bodies. Many people with bipolar disorder take a wide range of antidepressants and other drugs to stabilize their moods. Some experience no side effects when taking the drugs, but others do. The tolerance they have is partly controlled by the genes in their bodies' cells. In a similar way, it is possible that gene therapy will not act in the same way for everyone because of genetic differences. That is why doctors think that personalized gene therapy is the way to go. Neurons grown from an individual's own stem cells could be tested in laboratories for tolerance to different bipolar disorder drugs so doctors know which drugs to prescribe. By editing genes in different people's neurons, scientists may be able to figure out how genes work together to control what goes on in individual brains and how to keep them healthy.

Because one person's bipolar disorder is different from anyone else's, gene therapy will likely be personalized to best treat each individual.

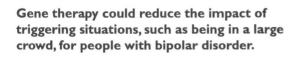

Gene therapy could reduce the impact of triggering situations, such as being in a large crowd, for people with bipolar disorder.

Hope for the Future

In the past, people with bipolar disorder were often considered insane. For example, in nineteenth-century France, the term "circular insanity" was sometimes used. People with the illness were sometimes locked away or punished to stop the symptoms. Thankfully, today, bipolar disorder is much more widely known, better understood, and properly treated.

Scientists are busy pinpointing the genes responsible for the disease and honing techniques of gene editing for possible gene therapy in the future. Doctors are becoming better at diagnosing the illness and devising better drug treatments. Educators are spreading the word about what it means to have and live with bipolar disorder.

People with bipolar disorder are now equipped with a toolbox of different ways to deal with their episodes. They can use a range of techniques to ease the depths and heights of mood swings by identifying

With proper care for their physical and mental health, people with bipolar disorder can look forward to long, satisfying lives.

and controlling their triggers. People can choose from a range of drug treatments and therapies to ease symptoms during episodes. More group support is available for people with bipolar disorder, sometimes through Internet forums, where people can share their experiences so they can cope better.

There is also less stigma about having bipolar disorder nowadays—after all, why should anyone feel ashamed of an inherited illness? This situation has been helped by several celebrities, including actress Carrie Fisher and singer Demi Lovato, talking openly about having bipolar disorder. People with the disease are often treated with greater compassion and understanding than in the past, but not always. To have episodes of mania and depression during your life is unusual. It can be frightening to witness and live through, but it does not make a person abnormal. Everyone is different and has different thoughts and reactions to anyone else. We all need to remember that people do not choose to be bipolar or have other mental illnesses—it is in their genes.

GENE STORIES

"It does really need to get to a point where we stop looking at mental health difficulties in the way people generally do: they're afraid to talk about it, they don't know how to approach it, and they don't know how to speak to you about it. Just because I have bipolar disorder, you don't need to look out for signs of episodes at all times. That's just part of me. Why not look for things we have in common instead?"
—Sam, age thirty-seven

Carrie Fisher balanced a glittering Hollywood career with the demands of her bipolar disorder.

Glossary

bacteria Tiny living things that can cause disease.

bone marrow A soft substance that fills the spaces inside bones, which in adults also produces new blood cells.

cancer A disease caused by abnormalities in cells.

chemical messengers Chemicals in the body that can transmit messages around the body.

chromosome Part of a cell that contains the genes that control how we grow and what we become.

depression A serious medical condition that negatively affects how you feel, the way you think, and how you act.

diabetes Health condition that occurs when the amount of glucose (sugar) in the blood is too high because the body can't use it properly.

diagnosed Identified an illness or condition.

DNA Short for deoxyribonucleic acid, DNA contains the instructions an organism needs to develop, live, and reproduce.

egg cell Female reproductive cell, which can join with sperm to start a baby growing.

genes Parts of a cell that control or influence the way a person looks, grows, and develops.

heritability A measure of a trait's ability to be inherited.

hormones Chemical substances produced in the body that control and regulate the activity of certain cells or organs.

human genome All the genetic information in a person.

hypomania A condition similar to mania but less severe.

immune system Body parts such as white blood cells that work to protect the body against disease.

mania Period of overactive and excited behavior that has a significant impact on a person's life.

manic Describes a person having an episode of mania.

mutations Significant changes in the structure of a gene.

nerves Groups of neurons. Nerves carry information to and from the brain and the rest of the body.

neurons Bundles of nerve fibers that carry messages between the brain and the rest of the body.

neurotransmitter Substance that transmits messages between nerves.

organs Body parts with specific functions, such as the heart and the brain.

phobias Extreme fears of things that do not scare most people.

prescribed Officially gave a patient a medicine or course of treatment.

proteins Substances that do most of the work in cells and are required for the structure, function, and regulation of the body's tissues and organs.

psychiatrist Doctor who diagnoses and treats mental health problems.

schizophrenia A mental disorder characterized by abnormal behavior and a failure to understand what is real.

sex cells The sperm and egg of living things.

sperm Male reproductive cell, which can join with an egg cell to start a baby growing.

stress A state of mental or emotional strain caused by negative or demanding circumstances.

symptoms Changes in the body or mind caused by a disease or health condition.

therapies Treatments intended to relieve or heal a disorder.

thyroid Body part that makes and stores hormones that help regulate the heart rate, blood pressure, body temperature, and the rate at which food is converted into energy.

tissue A large mass of similar cells that make up a part of an organism and perform a specific function, such as skin or muscle tissue.

For Further Reading

Anglada, Tracy. *Brandon and the Bipolar Bear: A Story for Children with Bipolar Disorder* (Revised Edition). Murdock, FL: BPChildren, 2009.

Balinson, Andrea. *Depression, Anxiety, and Bipolar Disorders*. Broomall, PA: Mason Crest, 2018.

Federman, Russ, and J. Anderson Thomson. *Facing Bipolar: The Young Adult's Guide to Dealing with Bipolar Disorder*. Oakland, CA: New Harbinger, 2010.

Leonard, Basia, and Joann Jovinelly. *Bipolar Disorder*. New York, NY: Rosen Publishing, 2012.

Poole, Hilary W. *Bipolar Disorder*. Broomall, PA: Mason Crest, 2016.

Schab, Lisa M. *The Anxiety Workbook for Teens: Activities to Help You Deal with Anxiety and Worry*. Oakland, CA: Instant Help Books, 2008.

Williamson, Wendy K., and Honora Rose. *Two Bipolar Chicks Guide To Survival: Tips for Living with Bipolar Disorder*. Brentwood, TN: Post Hill Press, 2014.

Index